She Speaks to the Birds at Night While They Sleep

Also by Hari Bhajan Khalsa

Life in Two Parts (2010)
Talk of Snow (2015)

She Speaks to the Birds at Night
While They Sleep

Hari Bhajan Khalsa

TEBOT BACH • HUNTINGTON BEACH • CALIFORNIA • 2021

Cover art: *TruthTelling* by Seva Bauer
Author's photo: Bader Howar Photography
Book design by: Russel Davis, Gray Dog Press, Spokane, WA

ISBN-10: 1-939678-88-9
ISBN-13: 978-1-939678-88-1

A Tebot Bach book
Tebot Bach, Welsh for little teapot, is a Nonprofit Public Benefit
Corporation, which sponsors workshops, forums, lectures, and
publications. Tebot Bach books are distributed by Small Press
Distribution.

The Tebot Bach Mission: Advancing literacy, strengthening
community, and transforming life experiences with the power of
poetry through readings, workshops, and publications.

This book is made possible by a generous donation from
Steven R. and Lera B. Smith.

www.tebotbach.org

For my grandmother, Sontina, my mother, Gemma, my sisters, Pamela, Colleen & Karen, sister spirits, known and unknown, who, like the raven, the nightingale, the enchanted hummingbird, inspire me every day to find comfort in the quiet of the soul, to always remember that to take flight, to dare to soar the skies, is the true enduring nature of the feminine, the Shakti, the dakini goddess we all embody.

Contents

These 28 poems were written in the early days of the Coronavirus pandemic of 2020 to chronicle the small and large moments of a woman's day-to-day, to express what was experienced as both real and earthly, as well as the internal, the spirit, the imagination that takes flight on the wings of birds.

Introduction

The poems in Hari Bhajan Khalsa's wondrous and wonder-filled chapbook were, as the author's note tells us, "written in the early days of the Coronavirus pandemic to chronicle the small and large moments of her day-to-day . . ." All of the poems, written in the third person about a character simply called "She," speak of a woman who is both unique and universal— both an avatar of a female deity and also just a woman of a certain age living an observed life in Southern California. Biographical details are scant; the inner life and its relationship to the natural world is what is split open and read the way mystics read entrails, the way scholars read sacred texts.

Early in the book we see the woman, this "she," "walk[ing] into the shadows/painted on her hand," and we know we're in for an adventure. Later in the book Khalsa tells us that "[s]he/isn't cowed by/the darkness," and that is one of the things I love about these poems: they confront the dark and the light of our lives. Even though "[t]he day has treasures/if you believe them," and "[t]he body . . . knows how to do//its job," she steps in and "takes a cool/ sip of sorrow,/doubts that it's true." There are no easy consolations here—no quick fixes, no euphemistic bromides. Just vision, and poetry.

Written elegantly and consistently in three-line stanzas, these poems are lyric meditations full of delightful surprises, like the "woman//in a rhinoceros mask" we meet in one poem. This "she" is sometimes awed with and grateful for the gifts the world gives her, and sometimes "the filling of her/place in this sliver//of the continuum/cannot be sated/with blueberries or bread."

But perhaps what impresses me most about these poems is that they contain magic. Here, in its entirety, because it is truly a magical incantation of a poem, is "She walks into shadows."

> She walks into shadows
> painted on her hand,
> follows the four-pawed

animals, the scent
that sways the river.
Birds on chiseled branches,

slung with green
moss, shimmer their wings.
A fish writes the sea,

eyes into the light—
tail, a prism
of motion. Trees

stand, suspended
by clouds, sun
blanching their limbs.

Night curls inside
its blackness,
scatters her chains.

The world created by this poem, and by so many other poems in this marvelous chapbook, is one I would like to inhabit—one I do inhabit on good days. It is a world in which "birds . . . shimmer their wings," "[a] fish writes the sea," and [n]ight curls inside/its blackness." So perceptively observed, so imaginatively rendered. So simple, so elegant.

Read this book; it will give you both joy and consolation to spend time, in or out of quarantine, with this "she." "She is/of this moment." I am so happy to have met her, to be sharing this strange moment in all of our lives with her.

—Gail Wronsky

there is an amazon in us.
she is the secret we do not
have to learn.

Lucille Clifton

1

She speaks to the birds
at night while they sleep,
in a language she does

not know, comes trilling
from her throat
like mist rising in a wind.

Do they understand
she is saying she wants
to know the secret

of their wings—
and if they love the sky
more than their nests?

In the morning
she washes her face,
her long hair, puts

on clothes, eats fruit
from a bowl. She slips
on shoes and goes out.

2

She walks into shadows
painted on her hand,
follows the four-pawed

animals, the scent
that sways the river.
Birds on chiseled branches,

slung with green
moss, shimmer their wings.
A fish writes the sea,

eyes into the light—
tail, a prism
of motion. Trees

stand, suspended
by clouds, sun
blanching their limbs.

Night curls inside
its blackness,
scatters her chains.

3

She places a glass
on the table,
it forms a ring—

dries to a crust.
On TV a cowboy
rides. Outside a dog

barks. A bell rings
in her ear. She calls
on the sky

to save the world.
On the screen the horse
rears, cowboy's

hat sweeps the dust.
She rests her ear
against the curve

of the dog, listens,
like she's saved
her world.

4

She takes the raspberry
onto her tongue,
presses it against

the hard roof
of her mouth
until it bleeds

its sweetness across
her palate. The taste
swims her back

to summer's long days—
skinned knees
and sunburned

shoulders, riding
bareback in tall grass,
sleeping with only

a thin cotton sheet
for cover, fingertips
stained a brilliant red.

5

She hears her mother's
voice as she would want
to hear it, like water

sloping rounded
stones, soothing her fears
and weariness with

murmurs. Her mother,
child of the depression,
a bride of war, never spoke

her own mother's
tongue, never learned
to swim, to bless; didn't

pass her cover girl smile
on to her first born
daughter—perhaps a slight

rise in the cheekbones,
the particular way
she brushes her hair.

6

She has ambitions,
but not today,
though she makes

an effort to read
a book or two of poems—
finds the words sliding

off the page into a gurgling
pot in the center
of her chest: Ellen Bass'

smashed garlic and cinnamon
season James Tate's
snake heads and chicken

feathers. Toss in some
hot dogs and baked beans,
kernels of goat teeth,

cut of pig femur. It
simmers and stews. She
takes a spoon and eats.

7

She says every morning
she is going to climb
those stairs over

and over, up and down,
until her thighs scream
and her heart wishes

she were dead. She hasn't
found a way yet
to believe she will live

forever. The little dog
in the elevator questions
why it matters, rolls

over, bares its belly.
At five she watches
the news, wishes she had

run a mile instead,
scans the screen
for signs of tomorrow.

8

She rode into town
in 1976, baby boy
in the backseat,

to a salute of palm
trees, hazy brown sky,
and what could possibly

be next. April pours down,
her fantasies spill out
on concrete, flood

the whole of California.
In 2020 she drinks
hot tea, discusses snowy

plovers with her son,
the El Segundo blue
butterfly, how it mates—

how traffic on the 405,
is so much lighter
these days.

9

She sits in the red metal
chair, face to the sun—
a spider's web glances

her shoulder, a leaf
loses its grip, dangles.
She does this ritual

as if it were, not sacred,
but a kindness
to herself. The scratchy

hinge of an unidentified
bird, opening of a door,
closing of a gate. People

run through red lights,
suffocate tears, bare
their shoulder of burdens.

She sets down her bowl
of thoughts, of panics.
It's four o'clock.

10

She recalls memories
in rivulets that eddy
into each other: Naked

and stoned at a rock
festival, asleep on the floor
of a painted cabin

in the high Himalayas,
stealing a can, or two,
of dog food,

her bride-flushed face
on her wedding day.
Last week, potting three

ragged succulents,
dark soil under her nails.
The picture of her father

in dress whites, tall
plumed hat, baton held,
like a promise, in his hand.

11

She stands at the crossroads
of her rage, decides
whether to shoot it

black out of a cannon
or fold it, tuck it
neatly into her breast

pocket and bring it home
with her. Instead
she gnaws off

the smallest bit
to carry into her future,
like the pungent

sting of cayenne—
sets the rest
down in the middle

of the road,
leaves it for the crows
and circling vultures.

12

She wants to eat
sliced mango wrapped
in parchment, papaya

with lime, anything tropical,
cool, sweet—libations
with ice blended fine,

trilling down her arid
longing. The filling of her
place in this sliver

of the continuum
cannot be sated
with blueberries or bread,

but still she opens
the door of the ice box,
hunts the forest of broccoli

wrapped in plastic, jam
in four flavors, bottle
of ketchup nearly gone.

13

She changes the sheets
on Sunday, like she has
for years, a way to keep

the days turning
in the right direction—
stretches the bottom sheet

tight over the corners,
snaps the top one smooth,
though her back aches,

wrists and fingers throb.
She folds and tucks
the military corners, a precision

drilled by her Navy-schooled
father, pulls the blankets
and spread into place,

props a flock of pillows—
revels in this small battle,
fought and won.

14

She runs her tongue
over the smooth
side of her molar,

ridge of its bite,
round of its gum.
The fan pulls in

the night's cool—
leaves out stars,
coyotes, the man

with no home. She
falls asleep under
the siren's pained wail.

Tomorrow doesn't know
it is, until it tastes
the sun. She has faith

there's a home—
it nests in her mouth,
not yet spoken.

15

She scrolls through
her day like
it's nothing

new, finds a door
unexpectedly open,
talks to a woman

in a rhinoceros mask,
winds up, at what
turns out to be

four in the afternoon
discovering she is
terrified inside,

but not alone. In
the evening, she puts
together a small

cart to hold her
papers. It is every-
thing she'd dreamed.

16

She yawns out
her exhaustion like
it's honey; sweet and sticky,

golden in the afternoon
light, thinks about
the tiny brown lizard

that sleeked its way
under her bedroom
door, craved, so obviously,

to be gone
from this foreign place—
lifted, by her husband,

in his cupped
hands, set free
in a potted plant

on the balcony.
The day has treasures,
if you believe them.

17

She eats too much,
suffers the churn
of grizzled chunks

of the eleven o'clock
news in her gut.
Memories her son

has spoken of
roil her small intestines.
In her gall bladder—

how she neglected
to tell a friend she would
never be forgotten.

The body insists
this will all pass.
It knows how to do

its job. She takes a cool
sip of sorrow,
doubts that it's true.

18

She wakes each
morning to song,
willing to let the rain

christen her
nakedness, to take
a chance that lines

of caravans will arrive,
scrawls of boats
and windmills

will be etched
in her sand.
She isn't sure

she can bear
the days when birds
don't light

on her head,
scratch thoughts
onto her page.

19

She hasn't found
the truth the crow
knows, its cocky

sway and razor sheen—
binds more kinship
with the basking seals

on her western shore,
bellies pressed
to warm sand, eyes

to the sea. There's no
divining the tides
on her map. Across

her chest a line
is drawn. Is she claw
or raised palms,

should she startle
and fly or close
both eyes and wait?

20

She runs her hands
through her hair, traces
the line in her skull,

along the coronal
suture, where
she and the concrete

once met, where voices
used to murmur.
Some days she hears

their echo,
asking whether life
is so worth it. She

isn't cowed by
the darkness, lets it
in, closes the door,

offers a cool drink,
a place to lay
its head, rest.

21

She slides the windowed
door to gray skies,
golden mist of pine

pollen, the amaryllis
breaking open
to its beauty–morning

and its choices
of how to start
the wheel turning.

A man walks his dog,
tugging for the grass
to be under its paws,

for the touch
of wildness. She has
slipped out of sleep,

eyes not yet hardened,
lips a corolla
of dusty rose.

22

She doesn't notice
that the bats have flown
out of her cave,

swept the skies
with their blackness,
picked up every voice

that echoes
a girl's dream
swung in the clouds.

It's not tomorrow
she fears, it's how
webs of the past

curl tight around
her wings. She
is learning to spread

them, to pry them,
feather, by iron-
plated feather, free.

23

She hasn't wept since
the story began,
a tear maybe, no deluge

of windows rained down
upon, mournful wails
of a chained hound.

She hasn't forgotten
the lake of sorrows
welled in the cavity

of yesterdays. By summer
the jacaranda will have
bloomed, rains fled.

The saguaros
will have flowered
their white communion

and smothering heat
slithered
across her desert.

24

She doesn't look like
she used to in pictures—
a yellow dress, a white

gown, or the lime green
satin with a gardenia
scenting her shoulder.

She always brought
home strays—hungry-
for-love mutts

and blemished boys.
They followed her.
It wasn't that long

ago she was her young
face, misses it when she
chances her reflection,

her so-many years—
eyes it in clear glass,
rippling water.

25

She writes her memoir
on the wings of an owl.
Pens the dates

of her birth, her death,
as she prescribes it.
She doesn't always tell

the truth. It's too swift
a labor and not all
what she knows.

She scours
the night for prey,
for a perfect life

to devour, alights
on a bough, bends
it with the weight

of where she
has flown, what
she has hunted.

26

She walks barefoot
in the dark
over stones placed

on the path
a hundred years ago,
searches for a sliver

of light, someone
to take her in, seat
her at their table,

give her food. It's
a dream, and still
she weeps

when she wakes—
yearns to be the one
on that precipitous

night to open
the door
and let her in.

27

She turns sixty-nine
tomorrow, thumbs through
her past in Polaroids

and brittle Kodak
snaps pasted in a flowered
album, scratched notes

from years of dated
journals stored in a plastic
bin under the bed,

deep in the jungles
of her hippocampus
where shards of memories

mosaic her tossing dreams,
meditations—the scent
of freshly mown alfalfa,

a glimpse of someone
on the street, who
just might be, but isn't.

28

She knows without
the will to sweep the floors
of rust and feathers,

run water over
her feet before sleep,
the days would

landslide her
like stones down
a hillside. She is

a tenuous thing, cotton
and moss, but still
she whispers to herself

that every molecule
matters and she is
of this moment.

She is something—
a singular
speck of ever.

Acknowledgements

For Women Who Roar: *#18 She Wakes*
Poet Lore: *#4 She Takes the Raspberry* & *#25 She Writes Her Memoir*
The Dewdrop: *#11 She Stands at the Crossroads, #19 She Hasn't Found* &
#26 She Walks Barefoot

Notes

Excerpts in Poem #6 *She Has Ambitions* from:
    Sous-Chef and *Goat, Cow, Man* by Ellen Bass from her book *Indigo*
    Eternity and *My New Pet* by James Tate from *The Government Lake.*
    Excerpt from Lucille Clifton's poem *Female* from her book, *Next.*

Special Thanks

Mariano Zaro: Friend, mentor, exquisite poet, for being the guiding spirit and champion of these poems and the process that brought them forth. I am forever grateful.

Barbara Blatt & Hilda Weiss: Our mighty band of three, who gather to talk of poetry, art, our dreams and challenges. You inspire and uplift me and keep me steady at the work.

Holaday Mason: For your wisdom, your courage, your voice in my ear to allow love, to believe in the power of kindness, patience and the magic of poetry.

Hari Bhajan Singh: Husband, companion, healer, fellow artist—always there to support and uplift me with your optimistic and courageous spirit.

Elyssa Ravenelle: For being the fierce and compassionate woman you are and inspiring me to always dance the dance of my authentic self.

The Amazing Team at Tebot Bach: Alexandra Umlas, Donna Hilbert, Cathie Sandstrom, and Russel Davis for guiding the creation and supporting the distribution of this book.

TEBOT BACH
A 501 (c) (3) Literary Arts Education Non Profit

THE TEBOT BACH MISSION: advancing literacy, strengthening
community, and transforming life experiences with the power of poetry
through readings, workshops, and publications.

THE TEBOT BACH PROGRAMS
1. A poetry reading and writing workshop series for venues such as homeless
shelters, battered women's shelters, nursing homes, senior citizen daycare
centers, Veterans organizations, hospitals, AIDS hospices, correctional
facilities which serve under-represented populations. Participating poets
include: John Balaban, Brendan Constantine, Megan Doherty, Richard Jones,
Dorianne Laux, M.L. Leibler, Laurence Lieberman, Carol Moldaw, Patricia
Smith, Arthur Sze, Carine Topal, Cecilia Woloch.

2. A poetry reading and writing workshop series for the community Southern
California at large, and for schools K-University. The workshops feature
local, national, and international teaching poets; David St. John, Charles
Webb, Wanda Coleman, Amy Gerstler, Patricia Smith, Holly Prado, Dorothy
Lux, Rebecca Seiferle, Suzanne Lummis, Michael Datcher, B.H. Fairchild,
Cecilia Woloch, Chris Abani, Laurel Ann Bogen, Sam Hamill, David Lehman,
Christopher Buckley, Mark Doty.

3. A publishing component to give local, national, and international poets a
venue for publishing and distribution.

Tebot Bach
Box 7887
Huntington Beach, CA 92615-7887
714-968-0905
www.tebotbach.org